Sistar, I See You

Writings Of Womyn And Their Magical Ways

Carli Rene Romero

Edited by Erin E. Barrio

Cover Illustration by Stephanie Preciado-Shelton and Cassandra Dixon

Cover Type by Sarah Pedregon

ISBN-10: 0692918124
ISBN-13: 978-0692918128

These words are for all the womyn who hold each other strongly.

TABLE OF CONTENTS

Gratitude

My Deepest Gratitude To:

Yvonne El Ashmawi and Monica Nadira Giron, who unwittingly inspire and encourage me to be myself each day.

Erin E. Barrio, friend and editor of this book. She is a dedicated force of articulation and support, who made this whim a real, viable and joyful creation.

My Dad, Vicente Romero, and the unnamed men who hold space for the hopes and dreams of women everywhere, even when they feel wispy and out of reach like - just maybe - they come from the stars.

Forward by Angelica Rubio

I can't remember the first time I met Carli, but there was something about her that left me eager to learn more. While I spent time with her, learning more about her, I still didn't quite understand her.

The reality was, I was still trying to understand who *I* was.

My interactions with Carli have been a part of this personal and magical journey of transformation for myself. A journey that is still quite rocky, but one that can only be fueled by the women that surround me. Carli is one of those women.

It is an absolute honor to introduce these words from Carli - which came to her in the same way words come to me - unexpectedly, but at the most perfect time.

As a social justice warrior, now elected and someone lead by pen and paper, I have constantly battled with whether or not I could be both a change-agent and a writer. *Sistar, I SEE You* proves that one can do all the things.

Carli's devotion to witnessing and writing was just as much a battle for her, as what I endure every single day, and it has been a connection that we both share.

This book of words is, put simply, a gift providing nourishment for a craving many of us seek, especially myself. The gift of being seen in this life and taking the time to truly see others.

I congratulate Carli on this beautiful herstory, that is, (in her words), playful, wild, tough, gentle, fiery, soft, and rich. Depths that live within all of us. We just need time and that special moment to unleash them.

~ *Angelica*

Introduction

Witnessing is a simple act. It is the act of holding space, deeply listening, wholly seeing another. Sometimes we are so urgent to *be seen* that we forget *to see*. I love to write and I love to witness. I have never combined the two in this way and was inspired to do so as a rite of transition in my life, and a prayer of gratitude to some (but certainly not all) of the women who have helped shape who I am.

I have found fragments of myself and the world woven throughout the process of painting these portraits and articulating the archetypes I see womyn in my life embody. These portraits are not meant to "capture" these womyn. Imagine that they are written in pencil and can be amended. Imagine that the names of these womyn may move around, each one choosing or finding themselves in different archetypes throughout their lives. Debbie Ford says that, "each individual carries the intelligence of the whole". We are each unique and universal. We each have parcels of each other inside of us, both light and shadow – magic and mundane.

I don't write about womyn to "limit" them to my perceptions of them, but to invite us each into our own archetypal magic, and the play of witnessing one another. Although, I am highlighting aspects of the mythical "feminine" in the ways they reveal themselves to me, each archetype represented here is available to ALL people. The feminine nature is whole, as is the masculine.

May you explore the different phases and expressions of your own feminine Soul - the playful, wild, tough, gentle, fiery, soft and rich depths of your Self as you read this poetry. Finally, may this writing invite you into your own magic: the art of transformation and possibility that begins with imagination.

Thank you for reading. Thank you for witnessing. May you feel seen in this life and take the time to truly see others.

A Milky Way Of Stars

I have blessed friends.
A milky way of stars wrapped around my heart,
each one of us beaming reflections in a continuum
of light.

I feel at home in my sisterhood.
A deep,
soothing
call and song.

My Soul is met and matched by the grandness and
potential of their beings,
their inquiries and desires.

Guardian Angels made manifest in a material world.
Chingonas galore in our mobile hood.
A constellation of badasses.

Thank Guad, you all show me who I am again and
again,
so I can't doubt too long, wait too long,
to rise into my own glory.

It would not befit your reflections to stay small.

Written For The Womyn Who Hold Me, Strongly

La Cantadora

She comes to me in my dreams...at 2, 3 am
lighting up my right brain
with weavings of magic, messages, dreams, tellings of
old and new,
mergings of ancient and modern.

She wraps her words around my bones, marking my
flesh with runes,
poems, books, writings on a website wall.

But her stories are so much more than words strung
together to review life's happenings.
La Cantadora doesn't compose.
She erupts,
flows,
is an infinite river traveling the world's many
channels.

She gets under the river floor beds,
sifts for gems,
wraps around stones,
carries life,
widens pathways set by nature.

She is a Weaver, Carver, Way Maker,
a path tread by the feet of our ancestors left for us to
complete.

She is linguistically alive.
She is all languages.

She is a network of memories moving toward the
future.
She clears my throat with her sapphire light.
She is anger, joy, sadness, loss, hope, belief, doubt
made seen.

She is the weaver of rugs we walk on...
or fly on...depending on which threads we've chosen.

She is our salvation and our curse.
She is what we make of her.
She is each of ours.
She sings the songs of our Souls.
She sings the song of the stars.
She sings the songs of our struggles and celebrations.

She captures the small moments in ongoing stories,
and the ongoing stories in small moments.

She is weaving signs in the night, while listening for
the sounds that matter.

Written For The Storyteller In All Of Us

Prayer Walker

Wisdom Walker, Way Walker, Prayer Walker.
There is a sleeping Maestra in this student.

Today I shattered from the trigger of worthlessness,
and then my Soul divined a healing salve in each
waking cell,
and I remembered who I am.

I speak the language of the land.
Medicine Woman
dancing her own heartbeat song.

I carry water in my eyes,
the color of rain.

My skin is Celtic.
My blood is Mestiza.
My bones of storytelling bards.

As I decolonize my micro-mind,
I liberate the macro-spirit.

My heart is awkward, but large.
How can it not be awkward in a world that has
labeled it as secondary?
As if it is not the organ bridging my reality with the
Heavens.

I am stardust organized in a woman's body.

Sistar, I See You

My nervous system will read a room,
tell me where healing is to be had,
guide my Virgo hands
to bring the touch of Madre Tierra's miraculous
compassion to body and soul.

I often resist this,
but resistance is not who I am.

My world is an intersection of webs,
of systems in coherence or discord,
functioning as parts of one whole.
My vision is whole.

My Spirit is an Eagle.
Regal and scrappy,
visionary and grassroots,
harking back always to the call of this land.

My spirit is #NMTrue,
melting into wisps of sky blue,
and resilient as a desert yucca.

I am awakening to the wisdom inside,
to the healing that sits in places.

I am praying my way into wholeness.
Silence is my refuge and my greatest fear.

I am learning to listen to the great unspoken
and string it into worldly knowings.

I am a young woman making my inevitable mark on
the world,
while asking that it be in service.

I am my strongest and most vulnerable self.

I am lifetimes of learning in one sacred vessel,
loosening my voice from its bottled neck,
and writing my way forward.

My magic is too potent to suppress.

Written For MySelf

Hummingbird Carpenter

Mama Cass,
creative lass
collecting an artistic mass
of badass feminine sass.

Soulful freedom is your paradigm.
She who expresses herself with a flavorful bliss.

Un coyote tambien,
Mujer New Mexican.
Beautiful mezclado skin.

Black hair with a grey wisdom streak
that sings of divine design in cosmo speak.
Like a milky way running through your hair,
a galactic lair
with a wizened flair.

Long and tall,
and legs for days.

Who says big feet aren't sexy?
I've got great planters for which to ground with
and so do you.

More bandwidth to channel the songs of Mother
Earth.
More leverage to stand tall in heavy winds.
Greater fins to swim in stormy waters.

You find the lines of stormy waters and draw them
into visual delight,
intriguing us all with your inner sight.

You are a hummingbird carpenter,
finding the nectar of different materials, both
experiential and dormant.
Bringing reflection into physical form through a
myriad of mediums
and finding ways to carve with spray paint, clay and
papier mache.
Chiseling expression out of that beautiful thing
which calls,
flapping your colibri wings through creator's garden,
and lavishing in it.

Thank you for your inspiration,
your play
and your creation.

Go on with your bad self.

Written For Cassie Dixon

Severe Heart

Deep feeling,
raw,
open,
honest.

You may be one of the most authentic people I
know.
Uncomfortable for many, I'm sure.
A breath of unpolluted air for sensitives like me.

You create more trust in a world that insists,
"say what you think others want to hear,
not what you really think."
You immediately felt a part of my squad because you
show up true.
Generous and unimposing,
simply naked in your healing skin.

I want to say to you,
I see the immoveable courage in your sensitivity.
I see a lineage of women who have survived pain,
challenge and journeys intense enough for story
books and movies.

I see your grandmother, young matriarch, taking up
the family helm and the sacred burden of leadership.
Guiding her loved ones across a divided peninsula,
and refusing the captivity of North Korea.
Risking lives lost for a freer life.

You carry a great feminine resilience in your blood.
You know this.

I wish to remind you,
that your grandmother's resilience is not sourced
from fear, but love of life.
That your ability to survive does not surpass your
inherent right to thrive.
That resilience may relax, bend, soften, create
openings, cross thresholds of joy.

It is a drive for freedom that steers your heart.
Your presence is rare.
It stays with me.
Moving and seeking,
there is a brilliant fire pouring through the shedding
skin of sadness that you're beginning to unearth.

I guess I also want to say,
you don't fool me.
Your power masked, or not, is unavoidable.
A quiet, compelling wisdom, a yearning heart, and
discerning mind.

I wonder often what you will do in this world.
What books will you author on psychology's edge?
What cultural shifts will you divine in a field
designed to "fix people" instead of draw out Souls?

Your blood is too vibrant for the limits of white
man's psychology.
Bring it full force with your woman's way.

Bring us archetypal wisdom and deep listening.
Bring us an inherent recognition of wholeness.
Bring us reclamation of our ancestral wisdom.
Bring us the woman who runs with the wolves.

Follow that "severe" heart of yours,
and sever the ties that bind.
Heal to the depths you see.
We need your magic.
We need your steady heart in our wavering world.

You have great medicine.
Let it drip from you like sap from a tree,
naturally, easily, in its own maturing time.
Allow the force that is yourSelf to come forth,
and grace us with your Soulfulness.

Written For Helen Kim

Converse, Spray-Painted Gold

Anita,
your name paints the form of a bright yellow flower,
with gold and orange streaks.

You are converse, spray-painted gold.

You are capoeira and danza azteca;
yoga near a cliff dwelling.

You are one down to Earth Tortugena, dear womyn.
An ancient one with shimmering skin
and buoyant youth,
like a grounded star
walking red mesas and desert plains.

You are the epitome of movement.
Flowing from pose to pose and place to place,
gracefully.

She who whirls with the wind,
an air-bender spinning her turtle shell like a
mandala'd disk
making the elements dance.

I am on my toes awaiting the unfoldment of your
future.

There is a red brick road leading to Emerald City
where you walk.

You are Dorothy and the Wizard in swaggalicious
shoes.
It is to the Queendom of an Emerald Heart that you
journey.
It is a dream come down to Earth.
It is yet unknown,
a flower, all its own.

It is for you, Anita.
Grace in an ungracious world.

A philosopher's stone,
dripping elixirs of stardust into the waters you swim.

Grandmother Turtle with her camouflage skin,
raising us up on strong legs,
and commanding us "walk your own way."

Written For Anita Lara-Beckler

Sunset Gold

A butterfly lands on a paved road
striking sunset gold on a black lane.
Violet weeds coat brown and green mountains with
the color of Spirit,
crowning the mountains with little crown chakras.

Reds, silvers, pinks and browns crystalize gravel in
ordinary driveways,
creating sacred paths to mundane homes;
and I think of you.

Kindness is written on each of these worldly acts,
meetings of imagination with simple surprises.
Kindness is a shimmer of hope on a gravel road,
water in a dried arroyo,
blooming yuccas against a background of plain.

This is your signature on the world.
It does not stand alone.
It glides across a page of plenty,
singing a story of courage, generosity and pure
cajones.
A page of Single Momma Super Powers,
of protecting children from homes that abuse their
bodies and stifle their souls,
of a woman of color holding office and
unapologetically representing her people.

Lady on the front lines with no weapons aside from
love and dignity,

holding out a handful of compassion in a blame
driven world
and speaking truth like it was made to be spoken,
with integrity at its spine,
reflection at its core
and vision at the heart.

You mirror the grace of purple flowers borne of
forgotten weeds;
of the lotus, risen from muddy waters;
of connection to that greater thing called love,
that we all have access to, but many times forsake.

Written For Kasandra Gandara

Boots Not Birkenstocks

Karla,
Ent-Sprite Warrior.
You climb trees not as a conquest,
but a process of homeostasis,
in equilibrium with their elemental lives.

You are the realist tree hugger I know,
not in birkenstocks, but boots.
I think somewhere deep down you understand that
tree magic is also yours.
Trees are so merciful they offer breath to the very
beings that pollute their worldly home.

Comadrx de la Resistencia,
you push back against patriarchy's norm,
willing to be uncomfortable
which takes courage and conviction.

I pray you shine ever-bright,
your mango colored,
heart-felt light,
and feel your love as your true might,
as you facilitate liberation,
and deconstruct suppression.

Because you deserve to be in your joy.

Your love is a connective tissue,
a communal weave
making friends in a plethora of places,

learning the branches of a community you seek to
know,
finding belonging in adventure's flow.

I see your sharp edges,
but I feel your soft lines too.
Nonlinear,
undemanding,
light that wields love through a warm embrace.
You give the world's best hugs.
Your care is fierce.

I have seen compassion overcome you.
It becomes you.

Your brilliance alone defies a *history* that seeks to
scavenge your light,
weigh down your flight,
and muddy your sight.

But amigx, your Spirit's wings are invincible,
and their Puerto Rican glow will illuminate a
shadowed night,
flapping away clouds over the moon
with a shattering Ancestral might.

You see,
you have a power I'm not sure you know.
It's a tremendous gift to the world,
if you use it.
Your welcome offers a sense of BElonging.
It melts hostility into acceptance,

strengthening and calming.

Feed your heart.
Nourish it with love,
like water to the trees you snug.
And watch your heart,
bloom and grow,
and new seeds it will sow.

Written For Karla Fernandez

Night Magick

I feel like you facilitate night magick.
Like, the way the moon shimmers at half mast
and stars twinkle of lives past
in a dark sky.

I see you in my mind's eye,
waving your healing hands like wands over beings as
they lie,
bringing old and new world songs of wisdom into a
corporeal weave,
giving anxious and longing hearts a wave of reprieve.

You are that mystery Queen in the Sky.

One night
I dreamt I was being attacked
and a Silvery Owl swooped her wide wings down
into my nightmare,
renewing my vision with light,
like a paint brush washing life over a dark canvas.

This is who you are to me.

You walk with such grace and mystery.
Sometimes I imagine a silver cloak like Gandalf the
White's over your shoulders,
like you were crowned at birth but just haven't found
your throne yet.

Your power is soft and glowing.

It enfolds spaces with buoyant waves of turquoise
and yellow light,
and a reflection of moon on water at night.

Your voice is gentle, but it lands with gravity.

Mother, Teacher, Sister, Wife, Prayerful Witch!
Damn dear friend,
I feel like you were brought to this Earth to mend a
broken path to palaces in the sky,
like your regal heart is here to help others fly.

Your compassion is what makes me feel strong,
makes me feel like I belong.
You see my gifts and call them out with a night owl
"hooo hooo" song,
and that is like water drops on petals that are dried
out.
That is like rain in a desert drought.
That is like night magick,
the soft moon shining on other's hidden art.

Thank you my friend,
for leading with your own visionary heart.
May you find that it leads you to new and deep
connections that are whole,
Soulful and strong.

May you know how deeply you are loved
and belong.

Written For Yvonne El Ashmawi

Death Midwife

Strega Del la Cucina,
avid seeker and coffee drinker,
pirate feisty, like gypsies of old,
trickster Sistar and threshold dancer.

You read and
walk between lines,
always sailing through seas of the unseen
and untold.

Colombian and Italian wrapped into one Kitchen
Witch.
You will nourish me with stories and stew,
and call me out if I'm acting a fool
like all good witches do.

We don't fuck with your cooking.
That alchemy's on point.
Just learn to receive and anoint the food
with prayers of gratitude.

You are not the usual unseen Seer.
You have traveled to death and back.
Creating a guide, Death Midwife,
with the wokeness to walk alongside
and hold space for those traversing the ends of their
lives.

You are confronting cancer like a boss.
I don't mean to romanticize, but I watch you, sister,

claim joy on a path
where you could easily pick up a cross.

Resilient heart,
golden hair,
eyes pooling a bright blue sky.
Witnessing others with a wink and a laugh,
you slyly implore us to fly.

Sometimes when I remember the truth of your
physical health,
unwelcome tears upwell,
but I know your Spirit is way more boisterous than
your current worldly shell
and your laughter and chides will ever reside in our
collective heart's well.

I honor you now in your truth because
denial is not your thing.
And I pray in the time you have left in this place
you dance,
you sing,
and in the way you See others,
you feel truly Seen.

Written For Tray Spencer

Corn Mother's Daughter

What up Protectress? Lady with the Wings?
Sacred Guardian of hidden and secret things.

I watch you dance through realms of life,
artist, teacher, entrepreneur and wife.
A quiet smile, a receiving heart,
always open to gifts of wisdom, art.

There is so much more than what you show.
Underneath your curious brown eyes,
lie a sea of wisdom,
knowing,
observations,
sight.

I know you See the spaces in between.
I know you feel with silent empathy.
Your spiritual sense is sound,
like a tuning fork's calibrated riiing.

I imagine that as you walk through community
spaces,
colors swirl around.
You remind me of Yvonne – our Night Owl Queen.
But her element is water
and yours is red desert brown.

My coyote Sistar,
Virgo-twin,
howler in the night.

You shape-shift to a black crow
at play in windy flight.

Gathering the gang,
keeping watch with a golden eye,
Corn Mother's daughter bridging Earth and Sky,
and whispering to the life all around
"Now Grow! Now Bloom! Now Fly!"

Written For Stephanie Preciado-Shelton

Makuahine

Salt Sistar,
playful like ocean waves,
swaying to songs of wind,
wrapping warmly around growing hearts.

Momma Magic Galore,
you are the quintessential
Makuahine.
Just enough humor and little bullshit
help you keep it real with all walks of people.

Aloha love is capsuled in your divine chalice.
Always a hug, a sparkle in the eyes
and just enough surprise at life's little pleasures.

You are down to Earth like NM desert womyn,
buoyant like the water surrounding your islands.
A beautiful combo of feminine magic
weaving connection in our worldly web.

A natural acceptance resides in your smile,
Aloha welcoming and bidding farewell.
Time is not.
Coming and going is the rhythm of the ocean
eternal,
and goodbye has no meaning other than "it is."

It is wonderful to call you sister.
You are like the clearing salts that you harvest
with sacred devotion,

delight and grounding.

Medicine Momma,
serving spoonfuls of Spirit.
Ho'oponopono to make the medicine go down.

Nurturing like piña on a burning sun's day,
laughing out loud with a hula sway,
beaming forth a Pele ray,
you invite a Soulful play.

Thank you for your mana way.

Written For Lorilani Keohokalole

Honey Queen

A honeycomb among cherry blossoms,
inviting pinks, maroons and violets into play.
Bringing rich and abundant honey-gold to a world of
wild love.
Oozing nectar that activates, merges and bonds this
community of life.

Maar-celll-aaa – your name sounds of a feminine
drawl,
lingering like the light of a summer sunset,
spiced with the transitioning colors of dusk.

Soft on eyes and heart,
making walls malleable,
opening Souls para recibir.

Truth, play, laughter – power soft.
Not soft power like weakened and played-down
power,
but tender directness, loving truth, compassion
delivering potential
carried con cariño.

A hand beckoning others to rise up like a Queen's
mandate.
Magnetizing magick with laughter and a curious
look.
Giving a forgotten language to unseen ways.

Shamanic Priestess Full Of Grace,

Carli Romero

Our Lady Is With Thee,
Blessed Art Thou Among Womyn
And Blessed Is The Fruit Of Thy Womb, Honey.

You travel like gold light in violet seas alongside us
in journeys,
Clairvoyant Pioneer.
Joining and guiding us to our own Soul's
underworld,
mapping cosmos from hands to stars,
shining sunlight on shadows
and reminding us that divinity is Ours.

You teach the spirit in subtle ways,
with whispers of love and grace.

You are a gentle healer,
connecting powerfully to the core,
through kindness.

You are laughter under a full moon's watch
and songs that sing the night to sleep.

Your presence soothes harshness
and allows the waters of life's lessons in,
gently nourishing seeds of growth
in newly churned soil.

You are the Queen of Honey,
bringing us back to our most natural selves.

Written For Marcela Veron

Like Wings On Water

Like wings on water,
you ripple waves inside of a playground field.
Loving, moving, basking in the inquiry of life.

Curiosity is your fire.
Wild and bold,
big with flickers of blue light.

You breathe life into the forgotten:
forgotten people, forgotten feminine, forgotten fun.

One time you held a pyre for the burning of shit that
no longer serves at your school.
You are one Radical B!

Queen Bee, with a buzz that meets the growing heart,
and helps it soften when growing hard.

Damn.
Rock on with your bad Self.

Sister from a Mermister.
Wings on water.
You walk into a room with play swinging at your
hips,
with authenticity that rises up to meet the forest like
a great Red Wood,
making Divided Meadows Divine.

I remember when you told me

the teens you work with are wisdom keepers of their
time.
Wisdom keepers of their time.

Dear sister, you wisdom keep the Divine.
Stay thirsty and stay whet
and refine, refine, refine.

Written For Jessica Vargas

Ursula, La Bruja Buena

I remember sharing a room with you,
priestesses in training.
We shared dreams,
talked of missed family,
missed mountains,
missed places.
This was in our Soul's time.

I am beyond grateful for sharing spiritual schemes,
mapping the unseen,
rediscovering magical means with you
in THIS Lifetime.

You are like a loving Ursula,
Pisces Queen of the Sea.
But instead of snatching Ariel's song away,
you call it out into the open.
Guardian of Mermaids come back to the Desert.

Nadirah means "precious one."
Precious like a pearl,
the only gem that shines on its own,
illustrious in its baldness.

Giron reminds me of Gira Sol,
turning ever toward the light,
bioremediating toxins,
bringing clarity to murky waters.
Girl, I see your Indigo Sight.

Monica Nadira Giron.
Our third eye chola,
visionary chingona,
who recites the future in her witching hour flight.
Bruja linda, almond eyes, heartful child – strong and
wise.

You talk to animals with no regard for the befuddled
humans who look at you like, "girl a freak."
Cuz you know your language is multiversal chic,
and that includes *Animal Speak*.

Creative genius con Virgensitas,
you literally bring dreams into the material,
the divine into Earth matter,
like a Friedalita.

Ages of Arabia and Mexico are channeled through
your *Feminine Mystique*.

I love you for your ability to See me and others.
For your child-like awe.
You hold the paradox like a vescica pisces.
Your beauty is bold and subtle.
You are playful, yet girl don't play.

There are worlds inside that heart, those eyes,
untold spaces where magic resides.

You drip life on the desert like a Goddess Sedna on
land.
Drops that shapeshift into snakes, birds, sapos,

populating our world with symbolism,
understanding, belief.
It is a light touch like sun on brown eyes,
that you bring to these Earthly ties.

There is a raw sense of Being,
and a clear sense of Seeing
when I'm with you.
The Earth is under me,
and below it are stars and a vast naked sky.

Our Souls are large and visions true,
and I have faith in who I am because I know you do
too.

Thank you for being my sister,
sharing dreams and magical schemes,
late into the moonlit nights.

Written For Monica Nadirah Giron

Our Lady Of Roses

Dear friend,
the only harp-playing millennial I know.
Your instrument sings through ages of survival.
A world's history of beauty and tenderness
overcoming war and brutal greed,
an instrument with no single origin,
rooted in the hearts and hands of all people.

My heart brims with giggles at your candid and
unassuming humor,
swells with gratitude at your humble service.
Meaningful-giver Sistar,
contributing through love,
holding space
and directing grace in action.

Thoughtful but not by standing,
convicted but not righteous,
angry but never hateful,
discerning but non-judgmental,
powerful by persuasion not force.

My Border Walking Sister,
Bridge Weaver,
belonging to the US and Mexico.
The real uniter of states.

You embody Our Lady in her uncanny ability to
dissolve borders,
with a love that gives no power to fear,

fortifying,
inspiring,
beautiful
and emboldened.

Hermana border walker
I believe your dreams are whispers from the other
side,
sometimes unwelcome,
but belonging to the great noche de La Luna.

Your namesake is Athena.
La Luna's great Goddess
beaming divine light in all directions,
loving Mama Earth as a grandmother loves her nieta.
Softening the shadow of nightfall for her children
with a great vieja's care.

Your Soul is ancient.
Your heart is young.

You wake blooming flowers in your cactus walks,
knowing how to nourish ancient life,
knowing how to be nourished by it.

You are generations of woman,
of moon,
earth,
ocean
and underworld.

I see the infinite life in your aging youth,

your thread connected to a deep subconscious truth.
You are petite and potent,
a paradox of power.

Radiant mischief.
Rose petal gleam,
the sweetness and mystery of scented spirals
made of velvet,
pulled by an ancient force.
Our Lady of Roses.

Written For Cynthia Pompa

Clay Womyn

Standing in the trees,
allowing a breeze to lift your radiant wings.

Clay Womyn formed by breath,
shaped by the arrival and departure of visions carried
on the wind.

Mare Bear, Master of the Care Bear Stare,
emitting pink-gold heart vibes from your waking
chest.

Your heart was literally cut open,
demanding a thorough eruption of love to unleash
itself upon the world,
saying, "I am flexible, enduring."

You could not live on this plain unrealized
so a re-birth of feminine wisdom occurred.
Doctor-God-ordered, in your Saturn's Return.

Bringing your courage to the fore-front.
Marking your Great Heart as the landmark of your
bodily vessel.

Leaving a scar that denotes undeniable love,
wholeness,
and a reminder to Believe.

You teach me belief
in myself,

in others,
in goodness and purpose.

You teach me laughter and simplicity
my minimalist Sistar.
That joy resides in homemade rancheros,
and Saturdays on the grass.

Partner-dancer,
wing-womyn prancer.

We've shared vasos de boos,
and dumb-boy blues,
ceremonial circles,
and healing truths,
and you've held it all with your Mexicana Sass.

Written For Mary Nunez

Mujer En Fuego

There is a tree outside my neighbor's house,
full of fire, bright red and orange, like a new day.
It made me think of you.

Your heart burns a brilliant tinder,
smudges rooms with the sage of Truth as you enter.

Your heart is spacious,
like your smile.

Warm and welcoming,
colluding para la revolución.
Quietly, slyly, side-eyely,
working flames of recognition into churches, schools
and city halls.

When you speak it is like Kali and Bridgett merge,
creating a woman that expands East to West,
and North to South,
creating a Prophetess.

You collect egos on your dangling chains with a wink
and a smile,
but you do it with fierce love and leave punishment
out.
That is your miracle.

The subtleties of your heart transcend right and
wrong.
They weep and water the fruits of evolution.

That is your grace.

Your power is striking.
It is that of a woman that belongs so deeply to Her
Familia and Her Gente
that it challenges all notions of division.

Though you've been burned by the flames of
racism's derision,
you scar with lilies and roses.

And when confronted by flames you harness them in
your vast heart,
where your bow of truth resides,
and offer a diagnoses.

Mi hermana, Mujer en Fuego,
you were struck by lightning as a child!

Given extra voltage for which to activate this world.
Given extra voltage to empower justice to unfurl.

It is written in your words, on your face, in every
inquiry and embrace.
You are a doctor of Truth in the world of alternative
facts.

You plant seeds of love, like pine cones, in a fire, in
the wild.

Written For Johana Bencomo

Magic In Mundane Waters

Witch.
Empath.
Organizer.
Strategist.

We know these things. They go unspoken.

What people may not know is how petite you are,
because your presence looms.
What others may not assume is how kind you are,
because your protection is so fierce.

You came to us on a winged broom,
in all your East Coast glory,
ready to sweep our clearing winds in spirals,
ready to join the crew of brujasitas you belong to.

There is solidity where my heart holds you.
Permanence there,
the infinite bond of strong women who hold strong
women,
of soft questions and hard truths,
of steadiness in the Chihuahuan Desert winds,
of showers like summer monsoons.

Water that comes naturally, as needed, without fail,
to clear and renew,
to breathe chaparral's hopeful scent on dusty lands.
Waters that are celebrated,
tears collected in vessels,

sacred rain made by women who are strong enough
to show themselves.

You hold space for blessed tears,
and then with a generous heart share yours in turn,
so your Sistars are seen and are able to see.
That is the generosity of a witch.

You are a white witch, curly dark hair,
eyes collecting un-named thoughts and feelings,
eyes that see behind veils.

You are a Spider Woman,
weaving a system of catches for the de-regulated
abusers of our communities,
holding accountable those who would receive our
votes,
but not our feedback,
those who would consume the Borderlands,
offer it up for a commission,
and call it a day in the Wild West.

You stand with brothers and sisters who walk in
kindness, love and courage,
with hope for simplified lives
as they face criminalization and deportation by
neighbors who have stepped on dignity in their rise.

You call to buried hearts with a bridge of clasped
hands that is stronger than any wall.
You name the truths that others may not risk
naming because theirs come with so much more loss.

You watch and hold space instead of claiming it where voices have always been, but just haven't been listened to...offering a healing salve in the ears of a witch.

You are thoroughly compassionate as you field through the feelings of an unkind world.

You are magic in mundane waters and laughter in dense times.
Sara, beginning in conflict and ending in Priesthood.
Your name speaks of transmuting power.
Of sovereignty.
Of Motherhood.
Your name is from God, Herself.

Written For An Organizer

Lakshmi Rite

Spring is appearing.
Spring is a soft glow on round skin,
voluptuous as color awakens,
delightful, magnetic,
illuminating those in her reflection.

Spring reminds me of your vibrant energy.
A citrus bite,
a Lakshmi rite
and the exploding sun at twilight.

Grace is your middle name.
Grace welcomes guests at your door,
bids them to sit,
let go,
lean in,
drop the walls,
no need to harden here.

Welcome,
pause,
soften,
open,
be nourished.

You are enough.

Even as I write this portrait of you
my pen has slowed,
lightly marking the paper beneath it,

because enoughness has no hurry.

Bounty does not need to rush.
Bounty is a syrupy,
quiet ease,
a welcoming into the divine.
A warm, wrapping breeze,
like a joyful, gold citrine.
You are our Yin Yoga Queen.

My brown sister with a Celtic Heart,
strategic inquiry smart.
You make recipes of love
and prep delight for expanding hearts,
making food a cunning healing art.

May you know your warmth from the inside out,
and allow your inherent well of light to eliminate all
lying doubt.

Written For Deidra Schaub

Carli Romero

You Grow Hope Like Your Abuelo Grew Chile

Agricultura de Vado,
you grow hope like your abuelo grew chile.
Red, green, orange in between.
Filled with mediums of heat that pack a potent
punch.
Power is like clay, molded by your practiced hands.
Shaped, softened, smoothed, calibrated to hold
justice por la gente.

Your courage is a life jacket for those drowning.
It commands the stagnant to swim in deep and
shallow waters,
so unapologetically
that we find joy in our own splashes,
before we even realize we're making them.

Stag Sistar,
Soul stance.
Your language is that of the Soul:
Soul of Individual,
Soul of Community,
Soul of Equity.
You are only just recognizing it as so.

Like Ishtar reimagined,
Guerrera Sacerdotisa with your Sacred Heart on Fire.
Católica with an ancient sway toward the original
divine.

Your inquiry is so poignant,

brimming with intelligence of spirit and mind.
Your curious leadership reminds me that this
universe holds the answer to every question asked,
that secret treasures lie in sleeping hearts,
that systems cannot be built or disrupted if we don't
first ask why,
and how,
and what are their gifts?

My eyes water with life at the thought of your
presence in the world,
with gratitude that it has crossed with mine.
Your persistence is a remedio for cynicism.
You forge stories of agency from acquiescent
narratives,
re-shaping colonial designs in the 21st century
and you do it with love.

You understand that righteousness becomes the
patriarchy,
so you choose justice and wisely forsake "being
right."
Teaching us to lead from who we love,
NOT who we don't.

Thank you for carrying a devotion to life,
learned by ages of ancestors.
For passing it onto your fairy garden daughter.
Your legacy is already written in her 8 year old
stories.
In shy wisdom expressed through lead on paper,
she is already making modern day art.

Like mother, like daughter,
chingona is smart
and she brightens the world with an Earth loving
heart.

May you feel sustained in the depth and breadth of
transformation you spread
as you steward a garden of purpose,
speak life into seeds with water and fire,
and watch faith in action transpire.

Written For Sarah Silva

All Things Inner Child

Warming sun.
Day break.
Long runs.
Feet over desert sands.
Crushed leaves in forest trails.
Rain drops on fair skin.
Beach sand in everything.

Everything outdoors.
All things inner child
and playful wild
and thoughtfulness that comes from nature's touch.

Huge salads scavenged from nature's bounty,
big enough to serve three,
enjoyed by your youthful metabolism on a nightly
basis.

I knew you in Las Cruces,
running on blue mountains and arroyos.

I imagine you in Hawaii,
listening to Pele's rumble under Kilauea's fiery
watch.

I foresee you in Nepal,
praying in lands blessed by a millennia of grateful
bows.

I think it is perfect that you council youth,

that your vibrant warmth will connect young hearts
to their own,
that your natural curiosity will role model inquiry
before assumption
in critically growing minds.

I feel the glow of your bright blue eyes
taking in delicious plays of light,
with wind whispering on your skin.

I am so glad you are out there,
somewhere,
sharing this world with me.

May you be near soon.
May you revisit the gifts of New Mexico.
Until then,
I'll see you in my dreams
and musings of good times past,
the memories of a loved one that last.

Written For Abigail Rotholz

Dance Like A Daisy

Earth-Fire Sistar, #NM True.
I see in you shades of desert mountain blue.

Strong voice, Warrior Mother.
Womyn with an Aspen staff.

You are leading ancient song in circle...
drums abound, rattles rain, dancing is powerful.
It demands the body to know her home in Mama
Earth.

I see you looking over desert plains,
sensing the Way forward,
feeling into the Way coming.
You will meet the Way with your Warrior Walk.

Shamanic at heart, there is fierce love in your eyes.
Your love is not afraid.
You walk courage into fear,
leaving it transformed,
creating a path out of the unknown.

Your Soul is a Preacher Soul.
You long to share your guided,
blue voice with brothers and sisters of faith.

Your words shatter glass ceilings,
like a tree whose roots have found her way through
false and temporary barriers.

Grounding in your connection to All in the fertile
soil of Creation,
growing, branching, blooming life into old
paradigms of rigidity and imploring them:
Evolve. Echo life and creation in your Service.

Your words unlock shackles,
reinvigorate faith,
witness lives,
plant seeds,
raise truth.

Your voice is needed and sought.
Filling spaces that are vacant of the Warrior
Feminine.
Your voice plants female wisdom in a male house.

Your Aries fire will light candles that hold hearts in
sacred light.

Your namesake is resilient, undeniable –
you are anointed with love of a flower that defies
cement,
life that defies containment and mortality.
Ever-choosing life
and the sun,
making man-made boundaries obsolete.

No Border will divide your heart,
because it cannot be militarized.
Your love cannot be oppressed.

Your voice is owned, solely, by You and by the
Divine.

Let it run free like water loosening a damn.
Feel your Spirit.
Rest in Her.
Let Her laughter ripple joy through your beautiful
body.
Let your body be the sanctuary that She is.

Say "Yes" to your ability to be silent and in service.
Say "Yes" to the abundance that this world wishes to
bless you with.

Know you are worthy, know your worth.
Know we are grateful.
Know we are here.
And know that we already see your Warrior Soul.

We will be listening for the song you unleash when
you're ready.

Written For Daisy Maldonado

Seed Whisperer

Tall beauty with rough hands
designated for those who work with the Earth every
day.

I love you so much.

I love that you are devoted to a vision of sustainably
sourced Earth loving deliciousness for all.

I love that you pay literally zero lip service to this, but
put forth the physical and heartfelt energy day by
day.

I love that you may be the tallest female farmer I
know.
Joyfully bending your long spine so that you may
whisper prayers of love to seedlings,
and plant them with hands that move the heart.

I love that your laughter is wild
and boisterous
and permission giving.
It is like freedom unleashed on a room.

I love how you hippicopter on a dance floor,
and tap your feet to banjo tunes.

I love that you are a farmer, not a food snob.
That you have the humility to eat Skittles and drink
Dr. Pepper when you need something out of season.

I love that you would cry for good cheese
like a Wisconsin baby true.

I love that you are smart and kind, thoughtful and
generous, and seem to the have the "presence" thing
down pat.

I love that I could not talk to you for two, three, or
four years and still totally trust that you are "there."
You are in my heart, and I in yours, and it is alllll
good.
We will see each other soon enough and say what
needs to be shared.

I love that you were my first meditation partner,
that the magic of inner worlds is a seed I got to
plant, water and harvest with you.

I love you for your bluntness,
your no shit-taking ease.
I love you for your heart, which is as big as you are
tall
and as wide as your sky blue eyes.

I love that you quietly make beautiful art,
portraits and paintings,
and gardens,
and gift them out with a surrendered heart to those
you hold dear.

I love you for holding space and walking with
bushels of grace,

and creating your unique life, despite your human
fear.

Damn girl.
I am blessed to know you,
and encounter you when life will have us meet.

Just know, until then,
whether one month or ten,
down the squiggly lines of our lives,
I love you.

Written For Monica Hoeper

Siren Sister

Desert mermaids bask in summer's shean.
Sirens wave their hair back and forth,
long and glimmering.

Great big eyes from which the world is seen.
You look deep into waters with night-like vision,
bringing prisms of light to shaded scenes.

My concrete-pouring,
roof-insulating,
Cha Chi's loving Mersister,
your hands navigate the way things work piece by
piece.
Puzzling processes together is your trade.
Puzzling people together is your hobby.

You make others welcome in a world that has not
always welcomed you.
You make shelters into homes.
You are home to New Mexico's nomads.

Wine always awaiting a dance to *Florence and the
Machine*,
a bowl awaiting wandering psyches,
crystals surrounding wandering Souls.

Rest and rallies,
laughter and tears.
*"Come, come, whoever you are, wanderers, worshippers,
lovers of leaving."*

This is the sound of your siren
to the hearts that long for belonging.

Sometimes you are a pain in my ass.
But it's only a staple in the cushion that catches my
weary heart,
a temporary ache in my ear that is grateful for stories
of life, law and love;
only the burn of an onion from making a delicious
meal.
I welcome this with our unconditional friendship.

Mama, you are psychic beyond your expression.
Your grounded self will tell stories of sight that
weave through planes of being
if you want it to.

You are the spoken to my silent,
Virgo Sister of a different vein.

You have loved me through victimhood to agency.
Thank you.

You have allowed my famished heart to be fed by
colors of passing scenes,
and music from warrior spirits
in my dazed and confused musings.

It's the simple things that make friends family.
It's the straight up acceptance, otherwise born of
obligation,
pulled from some deeper seed of belonging.

Thank you for belonging to me
my red headed,
wild-eyed,
Siren Sister.

Written For A Friend

Re-Sourceress

You sow pathways for resource distribution to
underseen efforts.

You stitch partnerships with a dynamic play that
refuses to be remiss of the joy of connection,
even when that connection is for the Resistance,
for the decolonization of a system that has
successfully demanded so many people's joy.

Because joy, despite oppression, *is* resistance, as is
connection.

You share rhythmic leaps to embodiment through
creative dance,
making movement another way to redistribute
resources,
using movement to bring knowing to all parts of the
body.
Somatic senses awakening through play and
expression that says,
"Fuck no. You will not contain this shit, because
this Earthly glory of bones and flesh and curves,
this unique speech and motion,
this fluid magic is mine.
Keep yo pawlicies off!"

You resist in style dear sister. I know that doesn't
make it easy.
The struggle is real.

No one can really know another's demons, but you
are learning not to war with yours.
You are integrating them, lovingly inviting your
Whole being into service of this life.
Your demons can be useful.
It doesn't mean you feed them ego-ridden snacks,
but your nourish them,
tend to them,
accept the gems of your shadow,
and know that your commitment to your own
shadow will help our country transform her's.

My dear Sistar Weaver,
you spin webs of networks and net worth,
bridging skyscrapers and grass roots,
grounding wealth in hearts and hands that have
always and will always do the work,
because it is necessary,
because it is their call,
because they are warriors in a time where wars are
only slated against concepts,
making war's casualties victims of convenience and
economy.

You marry laughter with purpose,
intensely devoted to a life of freedom in being and
doing,
a life intentionally designed for innovative works and
mad hat tricks,
a life where revolution can occur at protests and at
the dinner table.

Where revolution is the evolution of love in all
places,
in our bodies,
and in our relationships to space and each other.
Where peace occurs in pieces and the whole
simultaneously,
where separation is used to help us to understand,
and absolved for us to heal.

You are a smooth sailing stone skipped on conscious
waters,
sending ripples of impact with your freedom's ring,
and sharing your third-eye wink through salvation
selfies,
with a witchy smile and some sovereign slang.

You are a Willow,
waving leafy tendrils of feminine wisdom over resting
waters,
providing shade,
brooms
and branches for wands.

You might be the hippest hipster I know, attuned to
breakthroughs and not just trends.

You are the Sistar that saw me through the grief of
my first heartbreak,
has walked with me through every one, since,
and has celebrated ALL of the miracles in between.

You are a wording wizard, probably from Ravenclaw.

We are witches in a muggle world together.
May he-who-too-often-says-his-own-name watch out.

Written For Willa Conway

La Mona Lisa Mexicana

You beatbox
while you plant beets in your garden box,
wearing your Guadalupana socks
and blessing your seeds with Guardian rocks.

La Mona Lisa Mexicana,
but rosier cheeks,
redder lips,
and browner eyes,
laughing at life
with a Scorpio smize.

"Heads Will Roll"
and low-riders will slow,
as you strut your stuff
down Cruceño blocks.

Remember when we made coffee for a living
and danced to the *Yeah Yeah Yeahs* every night?
Talking of different boys
and career ploys,
writing our dreams into life.

Community organizers in the making,
and cariñas for the taking.
School, then work,
then El Patio
where'd we dance to any musical theme
and turn a dud into a show;
rap, country or rock n' roll.

Sistar, I See You

You are that fearless friend
who will own an empty dance floor
and make it full.

Hilariously witty,
smart and Soulful,
wrapping movement and words
in a dynamic flow.

Alchemist and Curandera,
healing sister with a poetic flare.
I am so grateful for your sisterhood,
your passion
and truth-telling spirit.

Even when shit gets rough,
(cuz sometimes your love can be a little tough!)
I can't imagine my life being as beautiful
without your fiery wisdom right by my side
and your love to help me surf the tide
of this "*crazy, magical, mystery ride.*"

So here's some mint and jasmine tea,
to you, hermana, and me.
Two peas in a pod,
one brown, one white,
Sister-brujasitas in our maiden flight,
following star-lit guidance on a desert night.

Written For Mandy Orta

Burquestocated

A strong oar in stormy waters.
You, Cousin, know how to navigate massive waves.
Your life is like a lesson in "Yes, I can" and "Damn right, I will."
You make heart ache look easy,
but only those that don't see your colossal strength
actually believe it is.

I want to be a Mom like you some day.
I want to show up for something, *anything*, with that kind of love.

Not the kind of love that's so forceful it smothers
or so free it neglects, no.
The kind that is an oar in unpredictable waters.
It stewards,
helps to navigate.
You can lean on it and draw from it.
You can rest it in a soft current,
and hoe it in a harsh one.

It is the kind of love that starry nights give to the desert.
It is a great string of light
to guide your precious starlings.
It is immoveable hope in clear bright eyes.

You are something else.

You are a great part of who I am.

You trickled into my life as needed,
like a stream meeting the estuary of my heart.
I am so grateful for you.

You are more than a cousin by blood,
I feel that my Soul designed this life with you in it.
I see sanctuary when I see you.
You, who have built your own sanctuary from
scratch,
are shelter for others.

And you are allll kiiinds of sophisticated too.
Burque style.
Burquestocated. Put that on your *Scrabble* board.
You are smart enough to argue it into word-dom.
I think, yes, one time I did beat you at *Scrabble*.
I was only sixteen. You must have let me win.

My Mom always talks about how your three year old
smart-ass self would let her know when she turned
on the wrong street,
that you knew the roads of Cruces better than the
City Planner.
Your humor is sharp, witty and kind.

You always made me feel I was enough,
and yet you pushed me, too.
You pushed me by your mere presence.
Simply a woman, committed to her own best.

No one can a give a gift greater than enoughness.

It is like handing nutrients to starving youth in a
malnourished world.
You are a food bank for the starved esteem,
but NO bullshit.
Only real, authentic goods.
No tex-mex chili, just New Mexico Hatch.

I don't know how to say these things to you,
so I write them
in the hopes that if your stores of enoughness ever
run dry,
here they may be refilled.
A current for you to rest your oars in.

Written For My Cousin, Emily Gaffney

Fall Trinity

Sometimes we are three stooges,
others the three fates.
We are corn, beans and squash.
The Holy Trinity of this Land
and those that work it.

Together, we make my favorite dish minus some
cheese and chile.
Apart we are hardy,
but a lot less delicious.
Why just be corns, beans or squash when you can be
calabacitas?

Why stand as the Virgo alone,
woman unto her own,
when I can stand much more tall
by the side of a Scorpio Enchantress
and a Libra Magnet,
in a holy trinity of Fall?

I guess Mom was asking for a lot of release
when she gave birth to each of us at the time of
letting go and blessing the past.

The season where transformation is beautiful,
but to many feels bitter.

We are all quite good at letting go in our own
different ways.

One of us leaves like the blooms on trees after
they've withered.
One of us cuts,
like the tree's sharp and broken wood.
One of us retreats like water to the roots,
prioritizing preservation.

I pray we become better at the graces of Autumn.
That we live colorfully, and harvest gratefully;
that we cook and gather around fires;
that we ground
and return to Mother Earth;
that we forgive and leave any justifications for
resentment behind;
that we surrender and let the winds of love
and the prayers of our Ancestors
carry us into ever-evolving beauty and discovery.

I pray we find the hearths we will call home
and tend to them with loved ones,
and allow the warming flames to dance into us,
our God-given right to
joy.

I pray we live and love and laugh with the expansion
of Summer
and sing with the ballad of Fall.
I pray we know the stillness of Winter
And create in the colors of Spring.

But most of all,
I pray we learn to love our Selves

with the richness of the season we come from.

Written For My Sisters, Erica and Cristyn

Your Enchis Are On Point

Your enchis are on point.
Red-cheese,
green-chicken,
layered,
not rolled.
They are famous in households across New Mexico.
Known by family and friends,
and friends of family.

They feed us with fire and fat,
preparing us for the harshness of life
and warming us on cold nights.
We take them with us wherever we go.
Saying, *my Mom taught me how to make these.*
She is the best New Mexican cook I know.
Even my Grandma says so!

Your cooking is the service of a Mother
whose door is always open to those in need.
Everyone is family here.
Our home has extra beds,
but they are not so extra.
They are always full
like our bellies.

We are blessed with a Mom who has shown us how
to mother.
We have watched you put up family and friends,
put up with shenanigans.

Four children, and more children, running amuck in
our spirited house.
Wrapped around a kitchen, circling a cook at the
center,
nourishing our bodies with love from your heart.

You translated this love to your work,
channeling Mom as Teacher.
Creating a home away from home for your little
ones.

Winnie the Pooh, Clifford, Dr. Seuss, and
dinosaurs.

A world of ABC's filled with love.

Going to your classroom was like finding wealth in
an underfunded world.
It was creativity, play, attention and intention in the
heart of a child.
It was 30 years of teacherhood in a snapshot.
Warmth, welcoming and bright colors calling in the
imagination.

I loved seeing your classroom, Mom.

Building blocks, and reading rainbows,
puzzles and legos.
All with letters and numbers
for young learners
beginning their journeys of life.

It reminds me of how you taught me to read.
A terrified, traumatized unreader,
who felt letters were Mount Everest with no harness.
Helping me string sounds together,
a little late, but better than never.

Night after night,
showing me that there is magic,
in this technology of words.
Who would have known a little unreader
would grow to swallow books whole and write from
the Soul.
Thank you for this gift.

Mama Meastra.
She who persists,
despite bullshit tests and politics,
and kiddos who throw fits.

Mother, teacher and bat lady too,
if there was a bat woman it would be you.
Stella Luna in human form.
We are concerned that, following retirement,
upside down hanging could be your norm.

And that Basi, the world's most spoiled cat,
will one day find you, turned, a bat.

Because like children and students,
you love bats, cats and dogs.
I imagine if we had them, you'd even love on frogs.
You are the Mother,

you simply care for all
making us at home,
with a delicious bowl
and the warmth of your compassionate Soul.

Written For My Mom, Carol

Abuelita Bag Lady

Abuelita,
but you're not little.

Your Soul is a giant,
an orb that glows,
radiating through your beautiful brown skin.

My first teacher of the Soul,
knowing eyes and wild hair,
Bag Lady with many totes to spare.

You have been my foundation of faith, of magic, of
prayer.

There is some smack talk about Bag Ladies.
"Old, wiley, crazy women."
But Soulfulness often comes with age
and *crazy* is just society's term for that which it can't
handle,
doesn't always know how to converse with,
doesn't feel confident enough to really meet.

In that way, you are crazy, grandma - crazy wize, crazy
goofy, crazy cool and crazy comfortable in your own
beautiful skin.

I love that you are my "Bag Lady" Abuela.
That you always carry with you nourishment and
gifts.

Your bags have messages in them for your friends
and family.
Each one representing a local trade, a community
investment, some food or salve.
Each one representing a loved one you've
remembered on your market walk.

Bag Ladies are the generous ones.
The strong women with miles of grandchildren they
have held in their arms,
rocked to sleep,
prayed between covenant hands with God,
held in necklaces over their hearts.

You are Our Bag Lady.
You are also our desert eskimo,
with 5 jackets in 60 degree weather, "just in case."

And you have rubbed off on me, with your
Curandera way.
"Only drink luke-warm drinks or hotter...
eucalyptus always by the door to welcome the warm-
hearted strangers and repel the cold-hearted...
limpias con sal, romero y calendula...
yerba buena tea to calm the stomach and nerves...
elderberry and osha for a sore throat...
vapor rub on the bottoms of feet to run out a fever...
don't go outside with wet hair or you'll get mal de
aire...
say your prayers against mal de ojo...
bring an extra jacket...FIVE EXTRA JACKETS so
you don't catch cold...

sage to clear, lemon grass to soften...

Our Lady ever on the front porch, protected by
rosemary...
St. Francis to welcome ALL of the neighborhood
cats...
open doors...
a soft landing...
extra beds to sleep the weary...
obsidian for grief and protection...
Angels, Ancestors and Eagle always by our side..."

These are the gifts of a lifetime,
remedios for the Spirit.

They keep me.
They are with me, always, in my perpetual bag.
They are the gifts of an ancestry of healers channeled
through your stories to grandchildren.
They are the passing down of grandmother to
granddaughter.
They are whispers from comadres, and life's not-so-
easy lessons.
They are strength and resilience in relics of tradition.
They are Earth Wisdom, binding us to Grandmother
Turtle's back
and the Circle of Life.

They are the songs that remind us we are Earth
and Earth is stardust,
and though we are small we are grand.

No, you are not small, Abuelita.
You are "Woman Who Glows in the Dark."
Your Soul is a giant and so is your Mary Poppin's
Bag.

Written For My Grandma, Venethal

Shadow Woman

Shadow Woman is an ugly mother fucker.
She is the most rich being in the world.
She is writhing,
passive
aggressive
full of stories,
built around a line of pain.
She makes others what they are not,
morphs and shapes them into sinister,
unloving,
uncaring,
unfeeling,
beings.
She can do this to perpetrator and victim.
Shadow Woman is where the light hides.
She is love awaiting transmutation.
She is edges of defense and resilience,
quicksands of judgement and discernment.
Shadow is a little girl being told she is worthless,
because a little boy heard he was.
Shadow Woman swallows and saves;
is a mass of the untold,
is frightening and alluring,
hides and protects,
binds and liberates.
She swings bats and sets boundaries,
and wears a fuck load of hats.
Sometimes she sneaks up on us, stretching legs that
have been sleeping,
going nuts, bringing wrath to every corner of a room.

Sometimes she is slow, prolonged,
digging her fingers into deeply worked bruises.
Often times, without some space,
some breath
or light,
she flights, frights or freezes.
Shadow Woman is our worst enemy and our best
friend.
She is our protectress wrapped in thorns,
and what she protects, no matter how cruelly,
dumbly, or brashley,
is precious;
a bed of roses and a river of gold,
water of life in a creative world,
connection, intuition, inspiration,
a round world, electricity and the sun at the center.
Sometimes She shows us where to dig, what to
investigate, how to get curious.
Sometimes we let her consume us.
Instead of integrate, we internalize.
Instead of forgive, we oppress.
Sometimes we drown in her waters,
feed her fire,
get blown in her winds,
can't get up from her gravity.

Sometimes when we are lying deep in her darkness
we learn how to light up from the inside out,
and guide ourselves through her vast body.

Shadow Woman is women who would believe one
accused rapist over 12 women accusers,

and choose him as their president.

Shadow Woman is the wild, overly tamed,
domesticated eruption
of shit we're figuring out how to share according to
our *actual* nature.
She is our teacher.
She is courageous enough to hold us in discomfort,
and teach us real empathy.
She makes comparisons
so that we may learn just how futile they are.
She is me, she is you, she is the Soul seeking
unleashment.
She will not go away until we learn her, study her,
become and embrace her.
She is as strong as our denial.
She is destruction that bears fruit.
She is a willful, wild, and magical beast.
And she will cut you.
She is my comfort and my razor's edge.
She is harm when left untold.
She is a lion roaring for freedom, and putting us in
our place.
I am just getting to know her.
She is teaching me endings, and the long pause
before new seeds break ground.
She will inebriate a world with drugs and alcohol,
and be the rock bottom that leads to redemption.
She is suicide on a desperate night
and fortitude the next morning.
She is more forgiving than we'll ever know.
She is ours whether we like it or not.

She is us...

Written For Our Darkness

Carli Romero

My Goodness, You Are Golden

I would wrap myself in a blanket
of your laughter if I could.
Cackles and chuckles and crisp ha-ha's.
Our tummies all tired from glee.

My goodness,
you are golden.

I hope every girl gets to grow in the love of a galaxy
of Sistars
wrapped warmly around her heart,
guiding her,
guided by her,
traveling together into the realization of their
brilliance.

My gratitude for you is forever.

People always talk about Soulmates as if they come
in the form of a lover,
but I have never known a love like the kind I have
felt with you.
Fierce,
unwavering,
grounded,
wholesome,
trusting,
challenging
love.

Your love is so strong
I have had no choice
but to turn it in
on myself.

My heart sings of hummingbirds and yucca moths,
of chaparral and desert walks,
of travels down the Rio Bravo,
when I think of you.

Of moving mountains for community members,
and community members for Organ Mountains.

Sacred ceremony and being held.

There are womyn who howl like coyotes at the
moon,
and those that humm under starry nights,
and we who sit in circles on un-treaded ground
after giving our watery hearts to the land that holds
us,
whispering secret dreams and sharing bouts of
laughter,
as we soothe ourselves in the remembering
that we are really Souls
made from thousands of years
of divinely crafted stardust.

I try not to miss you all.
I know that love is so complete it doesn't have space
for lack.

I hope to meet women of your kind where I am now,
to further grow this network of magic that tenderly
fosters blossoming hearts.

I hope these women are as brave, as loud, as wild as
you.
I hope they start their days with Actions, and end
them with tequila.
I hope they can laugh and cry with equal might
and vulnerability is their language of courage.

I don't just hope this.
I know they will.
Because they are women.
And women,
like men, like birds, and bees and dogs and trees,
like all we see,
come from the stars.

Have you ever sat,
stunned
and incapacitated,
with the knowing that you are stardust?

I hope you have and I hope you will.
May it burst your heart wide open
for the world has a lot of beauty yet,
for your heart to receive.

Our sisterhood is like a pattern of Souls,
a mnemonic design of Akashic realms.

We as women,
have come to cross paths as friends,
sisters,
daughters,
mothers,
granddaughters,
students
and teachers.

We anchor our varied energies in different circles,
holding the eastern light in one,
while holding the western light in another.

In some constellations we glow low,
marking the brilliance of our sistars.
In others we shine bright,
making the constellation known.

We are held together by the Great Unknown.
The creative void of darkness that generously uplifts
our light.

Shadow Woman sits among us,
layers her cloak around us,
teaches us Crone medicine
and invites the suns within us to shine ever more
bright.

She helps the human eye identify where bright
guides lie,
by grouping stars as patterns in the sky.

And La Cantadora,
the stringer of stories,
helps us to play our roles,
with grace.

She asks us to learn the art of weaving
with attention to the backgrounds and foregrounds
as One.
She teaches us that *"where attention goes, energy flows"*
with the dips and dives of a storyteller's tone.

She is our great teacher of context and distinction,
allowing us to determine our own meaning from the
abysses and masses of cosmic gases we belong to.

She teaches me to listen for the wisdom in all of you.
To dance my own heartbeat song
and trust you to drum along,
shaping a solo sound into a melody.

Let us keep our Soul beats strong,
and know how deeply we belong.

Thank you for sharing this world with me.

You are deeply worthy of its love, its grace and its
divine beauty.

Love, C.

Sistar, I See You

ABOUT THE AUTHOR

Carli Rene Romero is a New Mexican, who is in love with the state's blue desert mountains and won't give up red or green chile for the world. She is invested in cultivating feminine leadership, and building community with love and creativity. She has a Masters in Educational Leadership from the University of New Mexico. She has worked in community organizing and as a facilitator of gender and trauma-informed healing. She loves to witness and partner with other young womxn from her state who share a love of New Mexico's land, spirit and people. This is her first book of poetry.

(Photo by Jessica Richey)

www.ingramcontent.com/pod-product-compliance
Lightning Source LLC
Chambersburg PA
CBHW051734040426
42447CB00008B/1129